GONE BEFORE THE SHIFT ENDED

The Unanswered Disappearance of Patti Adkins

Linda Davidson

For Patti— and for every family still waiting for answers.

"The light shines in the darkness, and the darkness has not overcome it."

—JOHN 1:5

CONTENTS

Title Page
Dedication
Epigraph
Follow the Author
The Gone Before Series
Disclaimer
Preface
Introduction
Prologue

Chapter 1 Patti Before She Vanished	1
Chapter 2 The Secret Relationship	4
Chapter 3 The Money	7
Chapter 4 June 29, 2001	10
Chapter 5 The Trip That Never Happened	13
Chapter 6 A Missing Mother	16
Chapter 7 Law Enforcement Steps In	19
Chapter 8 The Boyfriend Under Scrutiny	22
Chapter 9 A Case Without a Scene	25
Chapter 10 Theories That Persist	28
Chapter 11 Patti's Son	32
Chapter 12 Cold Case Reality	35

Chapter 13 What We Know for Certain	38
Chapter 14 Gone Before the Shift Ended	41
Epilogue	45
A Personal Request	49
The Gone Before Series	51
Also By Linda Davidson	53
Author's Note	55
Acknowledgments	57
Disclaimer	59
Notes on Approach and Terminology	61
Follow the Author	63
End Note	65
About the Author	67
A Final Word to the Reader	69
References	71
Further Reading and Viewing	73
Further viewing	75
Further Listening (podcasts)	77
Appendix A — Timeline at a Glance	79
Appendix B — Key People and Relationships	81
Appendix C — Myths vs. Facts	83
Appendix D — How Workplace Disappearances Go Cold	85
Appendix E — Appeal for Information	87

FOLLOW THE AUTHOR

To explore all of Linda Davidson's books and new releases, visit her Amazon Author Page on Kindle: Linda Davidson.

THE GONE BEFORE SERIES

*True Crime Disappearances at
the Edge of Ordinary Time*

Gone Before the Shift Ended: The Unanswered Disappearance of Patti Adkins

A factory worker vanishes after her night shift, leaving behind secrets, suspicion, and a case still clouded in silence.

Gone Before Morning: The Unanswered Case of Asha Degree

A nine-year-old girl walks into the dark before dawn — and is never seen again.

Gone Before Sunrise: The Disappearance of Holly Bobo

A young nursing student is led into the woods at daybreak, sparking one of Tennessee's most haunting investigations.

DISCLAIMER

This book concerns the disappearance of an adult woman. Some content may be emotionally difficult. Reader discretion is advised.

If you have information relevant to the disappearance of **Patti Adkins**, contact the appropriate law enforcement agency.

PREFACE

Some disappearances happen in the dark. Others happen in plain sight—during daylight, between responsibilities, in the narrow window where life looks normal to everyone except the person who never makes it home.

Patti Adkins vanished on June 29, 2001, after leaving work early in Marysville, Ohio. There was no confirmed crime scene. No abandoned car to anchor a search. No verified sighting after she walked out of the plant. Only a story she believed—about a short trip, a promise, a future—and the silence that followed when she didn't return.

This book does not claim closure where none exists. It is written to preserve what can be verified, to separate fact from rumor, and to honor the person at the center of the case. Patti was not a headline first. She was a mother. She was a daughter. She was a coworker people expected to see the next day. She lived inside ordinary routines—clocking in, paying bills, making plans—and that ordinariness is part of what makes her disappearance so unsettling. She didn't vanish from some far-off wilderness or a nameless highway. She vanished from the middle of a life already in motion.

Unsolved cases breed noise. Over time, grief becomes a magnet for speculation—half-remembered conversations, secondhand "facts," theories that harden into certainty simply because they're repeated often enough. The internet can amplify that noise into something louder than the record itself. Yet the truth, in cases like this, usually lives in smaller places: timelines that don't fit, choices that feel slightly off, moments that seem harmless until you realize they were the last moments anyone could account for

INTRODUCTION

A disappearance becomes a different kind of tragedy when it offers no place to begin.

No roadside discovery.

No last call.

No scene that draws a circle on a map and says, *Start here.*

In Patti Adkins' case, there was only a time clock and a quiet exit.

She left early. She told people she was going out of town. And then her life stopped producing proof that it was still moving. The questions arrived quickly—first soft, then sharp. Theories followed. Suspicion settled where evidence could not.

This book follows the known timeline as faithfully as possible, beginning where Patti's story turns: not in spectacle, but in an ordinary workday that became the last day anyone could confirm.

Because sometimes the most frightening vanishings aren't the ones that happen in the shadows.

They're the ones that happen while the world keeps working.

PROLOGUE

— *She Clocked Out Early*

On June 29, 2001, Patti Adkins left work before her shift was supposed to end.

It wasn't unusual enough to raise alarms. People left early all the time—appointments, errands, family obligations. Patti told her coworkers she was going out of town for a few days, a short trip she'd been quietly planning. She sounded calm. Normal. There was no urgency in her voice, no hint that this moment would be the last time anyone at the plant would ever see her.

When she walked out of the Honda supplier facility in Marysville, Ohio, she carried only what she needed. She did not clear out her locker. She did not say goodbye as if she were leaving for good. She did not behave like a woman about to disappear.

She simply clocked out early.

By the time her absence was noticed, the workday had already moved on. Machines kept running. Shifts ended. People went home. Somewhere in that ordinary rhythm, vanished.

What made Patti's disappearance different—what would later unsettle investigators and devastate her family—was not just that she was gone. It was how cleanly she vanished. There was no abandoned car found on the side of a road. No frantic phone call cut short. No last sighting under suspicious circumstances.

There was only a plan that no one else seemed to remember.

Patti had told people she was traveling with someone she trusted.

She believed she was leaving town for a few days, not walking out of her life. She left behind most of her belongings. She left behind her home. Most painfully, she left behind her son—without a note, without a warning, without a reason that would ever make sense.

When she didn't return, concern grew quickly among those who knew her best. This was not like Patti. She was dependable. Protective. Present. She didn't disappear without telling someone—especially not her child.

As questions mounted, one detail rose above the rest, casting a long shadow over everything that followed.

The man Patti said she was leaving with denied the trip ever existed.

He said she never planned to go anywhere with him. He said he didn't know why she would say that. He said he had nothing to do with her disappearance.

And yet, Patti was gone.

No luggage was recovered. No hotel records surfaced. No confirmed destination could be traced. The money she withdrew shortly before leaving added another layer of unease—too much for a casual weekend away, too little to start a new life.

It was as if Patti had stepped into a story that only she believed was real.

As days turned into weeks, and weeks into years, the case settled into an uneasy silence. Patti's name did not dominate national headlines. There were no viral reenactments, no wall-to-wall coverage. Her disappearance unfolded in the margins—another adult woman gone, another mystery quietly shelved.

But for those who loved her, time did not soften the questions.

A mother had failed to come home.

A promise had been made and broken.

And somewhere between clocking out and returning, Patti Adkins had crossed a line no one could follow.

This is the story of what happened before—and what never came after.

CHAPTER 1 PATTI BEFORE SHE VANISHED

Before she became a missing person, was a mother first.

Everything else in her life—work, relationships, routines—revolved around that role. She was protective in a quiet, practical way, the kind of parent who showed love through consistency rather than grand gestures. She made sure her son was taken care of. She planned ahead. She did not leave things unfinished.

Patti lived in Marysville, Ohio, a town shaped by factory shifts and predictable schedules. Life there ran on routine, and Patti fit neatly into it. She worked hard, showed up on time, and did what was expected of her. Coworkers knew her as dependable, not dramatic, not impulsive. She didn't seek attention. She didn't overshare. She kept parts of her life private, but not secretive.

There was nothing in her day-to-day behavior that suggested she was preparing to disappear.

She did not sell her belongings. She did not pack up her home. She did not make arrangements for her son to be cared for long-term. These are the kinds of details investigators later searched for, hoping to understand whether Patti might have left voluntarily. They found none.

Her relationship with her son was steady and close. Those who knew them described a bond rooted in responsibility and care. Patti didn't drift in and out of his life. She didn't miss important moments. She didn't disappear without explanation.

Which is why her sudden absence felt immediately wrong.

Financially, Patti lived within her means. She wasn't wealthy, but she wasn't desperate. She worked, paid her bills, and managed her responsibilities without incident. There were no signs of financial distress severe enough to suggest she was planning an escape. No spiraling debt. No urgent need to start over.

Emotionally, she was more complicated—but not unstable.

Patti kept much of her inner life to herself. Like many people, she balanced public normalcy with private longing. She wanted connection. She wanted to feel chosen. These desires, common and human, would later become central to understanding how her disappearance unfolded.

At work, Patti was well-liked but not deeply embedded in social circles. She came in, did her job, and went home. That distance made it easier for certain aspects of her life to go unnoticed—things she may not have wanted to explain, or didn't yet know how to.

She was not known to take risks. She was not spontaneous. She didn't chase adventure or novelty.

Most importantly, she was not the kind of person who vanished without checking back in.

When investigators later tried to reconstruct Patti's mindset in the days leading up to her disappearance, they found no evidence of despair, no statements about wanting to leave her life behind, no indications that she was planning to abandon her responsibilities.

Instead, they found a woman moving forward—working, parenting, believing she had something to look forward to.

That belief—that she was going somewhere and would be coming back—would become one of the most painful ironies of the case.

Because whatever Patti thought she was walking into that day, it was not a disappearance.

And whatever happened after she clocked out early did not align with the life she had built—or the one she intended to keep.

CHAPTER 2 THE SECRET RELATIONSHIP

The part of 's life that mattered most in the days before she vanished was also the part she spoke about the least.

At work, Patti was involved in a relationship she kept largely hidden. The man was a coworker—married, with a family of his own. To the outside world, the relationship barely existed. To Patti, it meant far more.

Those who later tried to understand her decisions would return again and again to this dynamic, because it shaped nearly everything that followed.

Patti believed she was loved.

According to people who knew her, she thought the relationship was serious—serious enough that the man had promised her a future. He told her his marriage was over in all but name. He told her he was leaving his wife. He told her they would be together openly soon.

And Patti believed him.

This belief didn't come from recklessness or naïveté alone. It came from trust built quietly over time, reinforced by private conversations and reassurances no one else heard. In the insulated environment of shared shifts and familiar routines, the relationship grew in a space where secrecy felt necessary and hope felt justified.

But secrecy has a cost.

Because the relationship wasn't public, Patti had no one to pressure-test what she was being told. No one to say, *Does this really make sense?* No one to notice the warning signs that are easier to see from the outside than from within.

By the time June 2001 arrived, Patti believed something was finally about to change.

She told coworkers she was going out of town for a few days—with him. It wasn't framed as an escape or a disappearance. It was framed as a brief trip, a pause before returning. She didn't quit her job. She didn't clear out her locker. She didn't act like someone cutting ties.

She acted like someone stepping into a promised moment.

What she didn't know—what would later devastate her family and stall the investigation—was that the man at the center of this plan would deny it ever existed.

When police questioned him after Patti vanished, his story collapsed the entire narrative she had been living in. He told investigators there was no trip. No plan to travel together. No agreement to leave town. He admitted to a relationship, but stripped it of the meaning Patti seemed to have assigned to it.

In his version of events, Patti's disappearance was inexplicable—but unrelated to him.

This contradiction became one of the most troubling aspects of the case.

Either Patti had fabricated a trip that didn't exist, or someone she trusted deeply had erased it after she disappeared. There was no middle ground that explained both versions cleanly.

Investigators were left with an uncomfortable truth: Patti had made decisions based on promises that may never have been real.

And if she left work that day believing she was going to meet someone who had already decided not to show up, the implications were chilling.

Because that meant Patti didn't vanish randomly.

She vanished at the intersection of secrecy, trust, and betrayal—where one person believed in a future, and another may have been quietly protecting a past.

What happened next would turn that imbalance into a permanent silence.

CHAPTER 3 THE MONEY

In the days before disappeared, she did something that would later become one of the most scrutinized details of the case.

She withdrew a large sum of cash.

It wasn't an amount so extreme that it immediately screamed panic or desperation—but it was enough to raise questions once she failed to come home. Patti didn't usually carry that much cash. She didn't have a habit of withdrawing money without a clear purpose. And yet, shortly before she left work on June 29, she took out thousands of dollars.

At the time, the action likely felt practical. If Patti believed she was going on a short trip, cash would make sense—shared expenses, flexibility, no paper trail. It fit the story she was telling herself: a few days away, then back to real life, back to work, back to her son.

What it did not fit was the idea of a woman preparing to disappear permanently.

She didn't empty her accounts. She didn't liquidate assets. She didn't sever financial ties. The withdrawal was specific, contained, and purposeful—suggesting she believed she would still need her life when she returned.

After she vanished, the money became a focal point.

Investigators asked the obvious questions. Had the cash been used? Was it taken from her? Was it meant for someone else? Did it point toward a plan—or toward manipulation?

No answers surfaced.

The money was never recovered. No purchases were traced to it. No witnesses came forward to say they had seen Patti with it after she left work. Like Patti herself, the cash seemed to dissolve into nothing.

This absence complicated the case in ways that cut both directions.

On one hand, skeptics argued the withdrawal suggested Patti may have been planning to leave on her own. But on the other, the amount and timing didn't support a clean break. Starting over costs money—far more than what she took. And disappearing without preparation, transportation, or long-term resources would have been reckless in a way that didn't match Patti's character.

More troubling was the possibility that the money wasn't for Patti at all.

If she believed she was meeting someone—traveling with someone—then the withdrawal may have been part of an arrangement she trusted but did not control. Money can function as reassurance in relationships built on promises: *We're doing this together. We're investing in it.*

If that trust was misplaced, the cash may have become leverage, motive, or opportunity.

Yet even this theory stalled.

There was no proof the money changed hands. No record of

it being spent. No evidence tying it directly to another person. It existed only as a detail suspended in time—significant, suggestive, but silent.

In cases like Patti's, money often speaks loudly.

Here, it said almost nothing.

What it did confirm was this: Patti did not walk away empty-handed, and she did not walk away prepared for forever. Whatever she believed she was doing that day, she believed it was temporary.

And whatever happened after she withdrew that money ensured she never had the chance to explain why.

CHAPTER 4 JUNE 29, 2001

June 29, 2001, began like any other workday for .

She arrived at the Honda supplier plant in Marysville on time. She went about her shift as usual. There were no reports of arguments, no visible distress, no signs that she was distracted or upset. To coworkers, Patti appeared calm—focused on the hours ahead, moving through the familiar rhythm of factory work.

Nothing about her behavior suggested she was about to vanish.

Sometime during her shift, Patti told coworkers she would be leaving early. She explained she was going out of town for a few days. It wasn't framed dramatically. There was no secrecy in the moment—just a casual explanation offered in passing, the way people announce weekend plans or short trips all the time.

Then she clocked out.

The exact time matters. Patti didn't leave in the middle of the night or during an unaccounted window. She left during a documented part of the workday, visible to others, surrounded by witnesses who would later remember the ordinary nature of her departure.

She did not take her car from the parking lot. She did not appear rushed. She did not look back.

That quiet exit would later become one of the most haunting elements of the case.

Because once Patti left work that afternoon, every detail of her movement vanished with her.

There were no confirmed sightings after she clocked out. No security footage placing her elsewhere. No phone calls traced to her. No ATM activity. No evidence that she reached a destination, met someone, or even made it to a hotel.

The trail ended at the time clock.

As the afternoon turned into evening, and then night, Patti didn't come home. At first, there was no immediate panic. She had told people she'd be away. A delay could be explained. A missed check-in could be rationalized.

But the silence stretched.

By the next day, concern set in. Patti hadn't contacted her family. She hadn't checked on her son. She hadn't returned calls. The woman who never disappeared had disappeared.

When her absence was finally reported, investigators began reconstructing that final day in painstaking detail. They interviewed coworkers. They verified her shift. They confirmed her early departure. Everything up to the moment she left work was clear.

Everything after was empty.

No one could say where she went.

No one could confirm who she met.

No one could prove she ever left town at all.

That vacuum—those missing hours—became the most dangerous

part of the case.

Because in that unaccounted space between leaving work and being reported missing, anything could have happened. And without a body, a vehicle, or a crime scene, law enforcement was left to chase shadows.

June 29, 2001, would never be just a date again.

It became the line dividing Patti's life into before and after—marked not by violence or chaos, but by a quiet decision to leave early.

A decision that no one could undo.

CHAPTER 5 THE TRIP THAT NEVER HAPPENED

The story told before she vanished was simple.

She was going out of town for a few days.

It wasn't framed as an escape or a secretive disappearance. She didn't say she was leaving her job or starting over. She told coworkers she would be back. To her, this was a pause—something temporary, something planned.

But when investigators tried to follow that plan, it unraveled almost immediately.

There were no travel records.

No hotel reservations.

No airline tickets.

No bus routes.

Nothing to suggest a trip had ever existed beyond Patti's belief in it.

When law enforcement questioned the man Patti said she was traveling with, the contradiction became impossible to ignore.

He denied the trip outright.

He told investigators there had been no plan to go anywhere together. No agreement. No shared destination. He acknowledged the relationship, but stripped it of the future Patti seemed to have been promised. In his version of events, Patti's statements to coworkers were inexplicable—and irrelevant.

The gap between those two narratives was vast.

Either Patti fabricated the idea of the trip, telling people a story that existed only in her mind—or someone she trusted deeply erased it the moment she disappeared. Investigators were left to determine which possibility was more plausible, and neither offered comfort.

Patti was not known to lie about her whereabouts. She didn't invent vacations or fabricate plans for attention. Those who knew her struggled to reconcile the idea that she would tell multiple people the same false story for no clear reason.

At the same time, there was no proof the trip ever existed outside of her words.

This absence became the case's central fracture.

If the trip was real, then someone knew where Patti was going—and chose not to say.

If the trip was imagined, then Patti may have left work believing in a future that had already been quietly withdrawn.

Both scenarios pointed to the same unsettling truth: Patti walked away from work that day under false assumptions.

Investigators pressed for details. They asked where the trip was supposed to go. How long it was supposed to last. What arrangements had been made. The answers never solidified. Everything about the trip dissolved under scrutiny, leaving behind only a promise that had vanished along with Patti.

What made this even more troubling was timing.

Patti didn't leave work and immediately get reported missing. She disappeared into a space where delay was built into the narrative. A few days away meant silence wouldn't raise alarms right away. It created cover—intentional or not—for whatever happened next.

By the time concern became certainty, the window to intervene had already closed.

The "trip" that never happened became more than a missing detail. It became the lens through which the entire case was viewed. It shaped theories, guided suspicion, and defined the emotional core of the investigation.

Because somewhere between believing she was leaving town and realizing she wasn't coming back, Patti Adkins stepped into a story no one else was willing to claim.

And once that story collapsed, it took her with it.

CHAPTER 6 A MISSING MOTHER

When didn't come home, the absence felt wrong immediately—but not catastrophic. At first.

Patti had said she was going out of town. A few days away could explain silence. Missed calls could be chalked up to travel, distraction, or spotty reception. The people who loved her tried to give the story time to make sense.

But time only made it stranger.

Hours turned into a full day. Then another. Patti didn't call to check on her son. She didn't leave a message. She didn't reach out to anyone—not family, not friends, not coworkers. For a woman who centered her life around being present and reachable, the quiet was deafening.

Her son waited.

Children notice absence differently than adults do. They don't rationalize. They don't negotiate with worry. They simply wait for what they know is supposed to happen. Patti was supposed to come home. She was supposed to call. She was supposed to be there.

She wasn't.

Concern hardened into alarm. Family members tried again to reach her. They retraced what they thought they knew—where she said she was going, how long she planned to be gone. None of it led anywhere. There was no one to confirm her location, no destination to check, no itinerary to follow.

That's when the reality set in: Patti hadn't just failed to return. She had vanished.

The report to police marked a shift from waiting to searching. From hoping to fearing. Investigators began with the basics—confirming the last place she was seen, the last person she spoke to, the last explanation she gave for her movements. Work provided the anchor: June 29, early departure, witnesses, time clock.

After that, the trail dissolved.

No one had seen her after she left work. No neighbors reported unusual activity. No one remembered her car parked somewhere it didn't belong. There were no late-night calls, no frantic messages, no signs of distress.

For Patti's family, the lack of evidence was its own kind of cruelty. There was nothing to hold onto—no scene to search, no object to cling to, no moment to replay and reinterpret. There was only the certainty that a mother had not come back for her child.

As days stretched on, the emotional toll deepened. Questions piled up without answers. *Why would she leave him? Why wouldn't she call? Why wouldn't she come home?*

The simplest answer—that Patti chose to walk away—didn't survive contact with reality. She had made no arrangements for her son. She had left behind her belongings. She had vanished in a way that required believing she had abandoned the one thing she never had before.

And that belief felt impossible.

For investigators, the missing mother reframed the case. Adult disappearances are often treated differently—given more time, more assumptions of autonomy. But Patti's role as a parent complicated that narrative. Mothers do not disappear lightly. They do not leave without preparation, without protection for their children, without a plan that ensures someone else steps in.

Patti had done none of that.

By the time law enforcement accepted that this was not a delayed return but a genuine disappearance, the case had already lost its most valuable resource: immediacy. The critical early hours were gone, swallowed by a story that had promised a return.

What remained was a void—one measured not just in days or miles, but in the empty space left behind in a child's life.

And that space would only grow.

CHAPTER 7 LAW ENFORCEMENT STEPS IN

When law enforcement officially took over the case of , they did so without the urgency that often follows sudden, violent disappearances.

Patti was an adult. She had left work on her own. She had told people she was going out of town. There was no abandoned vehicle, no frantic last call, no visible crime scene demanding immediate action. In the early stages, her disappearance was approached cautiously—methodically, but without alarm.

That distinction mattered.

Investigators began by confirming what could be confirmed. They verified Patti's last known movements at work. They spoke with supervisors and coworkers. They established the time she clocked out and the explanation she gave for leaving early. Up to that point, the timeline was clear.

After that, it wasn't.

Police attempted to trace Patti's steps beyond the plant, but there was nothing to follow. No camera footage captured her leaving the area. No toll records placed her on a highway. No hotel or travel records suggested she ever reached a destination.

The assumption—spoken or unspoken—was that Patti may have left voluntarily.

That assumption slowed everything.

Adult missing persons cases often exist in a gray area where autonomy and danger overlap. Without clear evidence of foul play, law enforcement must balance the possibility that a person chose to leave against the fear that something went wrong. In Patti's case, that balance tilted toward restraint.

Family members pushed back.

They told investigators Patti would never abandon her son. They emphasized her reliability, her routines, her character. They pointed out the lack of preparation, the absence of a plan for her child, the suddenness of her silence.

Some of those concerns were noted. Others were set aside.

Police interviewed the man Patti had been involved with. He denied traveling with her. He denied making plans. He denied knowledge of her whereabouts. His statements were recorded, his timeline reviewed. There were inconsistencies—but inconsistencies alone are not evidence.

Without a body, without a crime scene, without proof of violence, the case hovered just short of criminal.

Investigators checked financial records. They traced the cash withdrawal. They searched for activity after June 29. There was none. Patti's bank accounts went silent. Her phone stopped registering movement. Her life appeared to end at the moment she left work.

Still, the lack of physical evidence limited what police could do next.

Searches require locations. Warrants require probable cause. Without either, the investigation stalled in place—waiting for something to surface that never did.

For Patti's family, the pace felt unbearable.

Every day without answers felt like a choice had been made to move on. Every delay felt like the truth slipping further away. They watched as time—the most dangerous enemy in any missing person case—worked steadily against them.

Law enforcement did not close the case. But it did not accelerate, either.

Instead, Patti Adkins' disappearance settled into an uneasy middle ground: acknowledged, documented, and unresolved.

And in that space, silence did what it does best.

It spread.

CHAPTER 8 THE BOYFRIEND UNDER SCRUTINY

As the investigation stalled, attention returned—again and again—to the man at the center of 's final plans.

He was the last known person Patti believed she was meeting.

The person she thought she was traveling with.

The person whose version of events directly contradicted hers.

That alone was enough to place him under scrutiny.

Investigators interviewed him multiple times. They asked about the nature of the relationship, its duration, and what Patti believed it meant. He admitted to an affair, but minimized its significance. According to him, there were no plans to leave town together, no trip, no shared future waiting just beyond June 29.

When questioned about the money Patti had withdrawn, he denied receiving any of it. When asked where Patti might have gone, he said he didn't know. When pressed on why she would tell others she was traveling with him if that wasn't true, his answers offered no clarity.

His timeline was reviewed. His movements that day were examined as closely as possible. But without a body or a crime scene, investigators were limited in what they could prove. Suspicion, however strong, could not substitute for evidence.

And evidence never surfaced.

What troubled those closest to Patti—and continues to trouble observers of the case—was not just what the man said, but what he didn't. There was no urgency in his public statements. No visible effort to search for her. No sustained appeal for information. His life continued largely uninterrupted.

For Patti's family, this absence of concern felt deafening.

They believed Patti had trusted him with her future. They believed she had acted on promises he had made. And yet, when she vanished, he appeared detached from the consequences of that trust.

Still, law enforcement could not move forward without something concrete.

People of interest are not suspects.

Suspicions are not proof.

Belief is not evidence.

The man was never charged. He was never arrested. He remained —legally—just another person questioned in an unresolved disappearance.

That distinction created a painful divide.

On one side were those who felt the truth was obvious, even if it couldn't be proven. On the other was a justice system bound by standards that Patti's case simply couldn't meet.

As months turned into years, scrutiny faded into background

noise. Interviews stopped. Leads dried up. The man at the center of the storm returned to anonymity, while Patti's family remained suspended in uncertainty.

The imbalance was stark.

One life moved forward.

One life stood still.

And somewhere between what could be said and what could be proven, the truth about Patti Adkins remained locked away—out of reach, but not out of mind.

CHAPTER 9 A CASE WITHOUT A SCENE

In most disappearances that turn criminal, there is a place investigators can return to again and again.

A road shoulder.

A home.

A vehicle.

A patch of ground where something went wrong.

In the case of , there was nothing.

No abandoned car.

No damaged property.

No trail that could be walked or mapped.

The absence of a crime scene became one of the investigation's greatest obstacles—and one of its most unsettling features.

Patti did not vanish in a moment of visible chaos. She did not leave behind signs of a struggle or an interrupted routine. She disappeared cleanly, between known points, in a way that offered no physical anchor for law enforcement to build around.

This meant no search perimeter could be established.

No forensic teams could be deployed with purpose.

No evidence could be processed, reprocessed, or revisited.

Without a scene, there was no starting point—only an ending.

Investigators were left working backward from nothing. They reconstructed conversations. They analyzed timelines. They compared statements. But each path led to the same dead end: Patti's last confirmed location was work, and nothing tied her to any place after that.

This lack of physical evidence also limited investigative authority. Warrants require probable cause. Searches require locations. Without either, law enforcement could not compel cooperation beyond interviews or voluntary statements.

Suspicion lingered, but suspicion cannot unlock doors.

Over time, the case took on the quiet characteristics of many unresolved adult disappearances. Files grew thicker with notes, not breakthroughs. Leads were logged, not pursued. The case remained open, but inactive—waiting for a spark that never arrived.

For Patti's family, the lack of a crime scene was its own kind of torment. There was no place to grieve, no ground to search, no location that held the weight of what had been lost. Patti hadn't disappeared from a place—they had lost her from time itself.

Even years later, investigators acknowledged the same truth: if Patti's disappearance involved foul play, it was executed with a level of control that left nothing behind. No witnesses. No trace. No mistake that could later be corrected.

And if it did not involve foul play—if Patti had somehow walked away on her own—then she had done so in a way that erased her entire life without leaving a single footprint.

Both possibilities felt equally implausible.

Cases without scenes do not fade because they are solved. They fade because there is nowhere left to look.

And yet, Patti Adkins' disappearance refuses to settle into obscurity—not because of what was found, but because of what never was.

A life vanished.

A mother gone.

And a case built entirely on absence.

CHAPTER 10
THEORIES THAT PERSIST

When evidence is scarce, theories multiply.

In the case of , explanations filled the space where answers should have been—some offered quietly by investigators, others argued passionately by those who refused to let her disappearance be dismissed as choice or chance.

Each theory tried to explain the same impossible fact: a devoted mother vanished without a trace.

The Voluntary Disappearance Theory

This was the earliest—and most damaging—assumption.

Patti was an adult. She left work on her own. She withdrew cash. On paper, those details suggested autonomy. Some believed she chose to walk away from her life, possibly to start over.

But this theory collapsed under scrutiny.

Patti made no arrangements for her son. She left behind her belongings, her home, her responsibilities. She didn't access her bank accounts after June 29. She didn't surface under another identity. No sightings, no confirmed contact, no trace of reinvention ever appeared.

Walking away requires planning.

Patti had none.

The Planned Trip Gone Wrong

Another theory suggested Patti did leave voluntarily—but encountered trouble shortly after.

Perhaps she met the person she believed she was traveling with. Perhaps she realized the promises weren't real. Perhaps an argument escalated. Perhaps the situation turned dangerous.

This explanation accounted for several facts:
- The cash withdrawal
- The expectation of travel
- The immediate disappearance after leaving work

But it relied on one assumption that could never be proven—that the trip was real.

Without confirmation that Patti met anyone after work, the theory remained suspended, plausible but unsupported.

Foul Play and Concealment

For many, this theory felt unavoidable.

Patti trusted someone. That trust may have placed her in a

vulnerable position. If violence occurred, it happened somewhere controlled—somewhere no witnesses could intervene and no evidence would remain.

This theory explained the clean disappearance.

It explained the silence.

It explained the lack of a body.

But it also raised the hardest question of all: *how does someone commit a crime so complete that nothing surfaces afterward?*

Without a crime scene, this explanation could never move beyond suspicion.

Why None of Them Resolve the Case

Each theory answered one question and created five more.

If Patti left willingly, why abandon her son?

If she planned a trip, why did no one else acknowledge it?

If someone harmed her, how did they leave no trace?

Theories persisted not because they were convincing, but because the truth remained unreachable.

Over time, speculation became a substitute for progress. The case lived on in fragments—half-beliefs, unresolved narratives, and quiet debates that never led to action.

What all the theories shared was one central flaw: none of them could explain Patti Adkins as she was known to be.

She was not impulsive.

She was not careless.

She was not disposable.

And whatever happened to her did not fit neatly into any explanation offered so far.

Theories persist because hope persists—that one of them, someday, will finally align with a fact strong enough to change everything.

Until then, they remain what they have always been.

Attempts to make sense of silence.

CHAPTER 11
PATTI'S SON

For 's son, the disappearance was not a mystery to be analyzed. It was a rupture—sudden, permanent, and impossible to explain.

One day, his mother was there. The next, she wasn't.

There was no warning. No goodbye. No moment he could return to and rethink. She didn't say she was leaving. She didn't promise she'd be back later that night. She simply failed to come home, and in doing so, left behind a silence that would stretch across years.

Children experience loss differently. They do not frame it in theories or timelines. They feel it in absence—in the empty space where a voice should be, in routines that suddenly collapse. Patti's son was left to navigate questions he was too young to answer and emotions no one could resolve for him.

Why didn't she come back?

Why didn't she call?

Why did she leave me?

Those questions followed him as he grew older, reshaping themselves with each passing year. What begins as confusion hardens into something heavier—a need for truth that never finds a place to land.

Family members stepped in where they could. Life continued in the way it must. But nothing replaces a parent, and nothing softens the knowledge that the person who loved you most vanished without explanation.

As Patti's case stalled, the weight shifted quietly onto those left behind. Her son grew up in the shadow of uncertainty, carrying not just grief, but the unresolved nature of it. There was no grave to visit. No answers to lean on. Only the knowledge that his mother's story had been interrupted—and that no one could tell him how it ended.

Over time, the public attention faded. Leads dried up. The case moved further from headlines and closer to being forgotten. But for Patti's son, it never moved at all.

Every milestone—birthdays, graduations, moments Patti should have witnessed—became reminders of what was missing. The years did not make the loss easier; they made it more complex. As he grew old enough to understand the circumstances of her disappearance, new questions emerged, sharper and more painful than the ones before.

Could she have chosen to leave?

Could she have been deceived?

Could someone have taken her away from him?

Each possibility carried its own kind of grief.

For families of the missing, time does not heal in the way people expect. It stretches. It settles into daily life. It becomes something you carry rather than something you move past.

Patti's son did not lose his mother to a moment he could mourn.

He lost her to uncertainty.

LINDA DAVIDSON

And that uncertainty—quiet, unresolved, and enduring—became part of who he was forced to become.

CHAPTER 12 COLD CASE REALITY

As months turned into years, the disappearance of settled into a category no family ever wants to hear: *cold case*.

The term sounds procedural, almost neutral. In reality, it signals something far more painful—that the obvious leads have been exhausted, the early momentum lost, and the investigation now survives on patience rather than urgency.

For Patti's family, the shift was unmistakable.

Calls from investigators became less frequent. Updates grew sparse. What once felt like an active search began to resemble quiet maintenance—files preserved, notes revisited occasionally, but no clear path forward. The case was not closed, but it was no longer moving.

Cold cases do not go silent because they lack importance. They go silent because they lack leverage.

In Patti's case, the same obstacles remained immovable. There was still no body. No confirmed crime scene. No witnesses who could place her anywhere after she left work. No physical evidence strong enough to justify new warrants or compel cooperation.

Time, meanwhile, worked against everything else.

Memories faded. People moved away. Details that once felt sharp blurred at the edges. Even small inconsistencies—once potentially meaningful—became harder to interpret as the context around them dissolved.

Investigators acknowledged privately what families of the missing learn painfully fast: without new information, cases like Patti's rely on one of three things to move forward.

A confession.

A discovery.

Or a mistake made long after the fact.

None of those had happened.

Still, the case was not abandoned. Patti Adkins' file remained open, revisited periodically as cold case units changed hands or new eyes reviewed old material. Her name surfaced again when similar disappearances were discussed, when patterns were reexamined, when the question of how adults vanish without a trace came back into focus.

But revisiting a case is not the same as advancing it.

For law enforcement, cold cases require restraint as much as persistence. Accusations cannot be made without proof. Pressure cannot be applied without cause. Even when suspicion feels obvious, the legal system demands certainty it cannot provide.

For families, that restraint feels like paralysis.

They live with the knowledge that answers may exist—but may never surface. That someone may know exactly what happened to Patti and simply never speak. That the truth could remain hidden not because it is complex, but because it is inconvenient.

Cold case reality is this: the passage of time does not clarify—it complicates.

And yet, time is not only an enemy.

It can also loosen tongues.

It can erode loyalties.

It can make silence heavier than confession.

This is the space Patti Adkins' case now occupies—not resolved, not forgotten, but waiting. Suspended between what is known and what has yet to be said.

A cold case is not the end of a story.

It is the longest pause imaginable.

CHAPTER 13 WHAT WE KNOW FOR CERTAIN

In a case defined by uncertainty, there are still facts that do not bend.

They are the fixed points investigators return to, the pieces that have remained unchanged no matter how much time has passed. In the disappearance of , those certainties are few—but they matter.

Patti went to work on June 29, 2001.

She left early.

And she was never seen again.

That timeline has never been disputed.

She told coworkers she was going out of town for a few days. Multiple people heard the same explanation. This was not a misunderstanding or a single misremembered conversation. Patti presented a consistent story in the hours before she vanished.

Whatever happened after she left work did not interrupt her midshift. There was no emergency call. No confrontation witnessed. She walked out under ordinary circumstances.

Patti withdrew a significant amount of cash shortly before disappearing. The money has never been recovered. There is no record of it being spent, deposited, or transferred. Its absence remains unexplained.

She did not take most of her belongings.

She did not pack for a long-term absence.

She did not arrange care for her son.

Those omissions speak loudly.

Patti's bank accounts went quiet. Her phone activity stopped. She did not surface elsewhere under her own name or another identity. No confirmed sightings have ever placed her alive after June 29.

The man she believed she was traveling with denied the trip existed. He acknowledged the relationship but rejected the future Patti seemed to be acting on. This contradiction has never been resolved.

Law enforcement investigated and questioned those closest to her. No arrests were made. No charges filed. No official determination of what happened to Patti has ever been announced.

The case remains open.

Taken together, these facts narrow the field without closing it.

They tell us Patti did not prepare to abandon her life.

They tell us she believed she was going somewhere—and coming back.

They tell us someone knows more than they have said.

What they do not tell us is where Patti went after she left work, who she met, or what happened in the hours that followed. The gap between her departure and her disappearance remains unfilled.

In many cases, uncertainty comes from conflicting evidence.

Here, it comes from the absence of it.

What is known stands firm.

What is unknown casts a long shadow.

And between those two truths lies the unanswered question that has defined this case for more than two decades:

How does a mother disappear so completely—without leaving a single trace behind?

CHAPTER 14 GONE BEFORE THE SHIFT ENDED

Timing is not just a detail in this case.

It is the spine of it.

Patti Adkins did not disappear in the dead of night or in a moment of visible danger. She vanished in daylight, during working hours, between responsibilities—between clocking out and coming home. That narrow window is what makes her disappearance so difficult to reconcile.

She left work early, believing she was stepping into something planned and temporary. She did not rush. She did not flee. She did not leave as someone cutting ties. She left as someone who expected to return.

That expectation is what haunts this case.

Because it suggests Patti's disappearance did not begin with fear or desperation. It began with trust.

The title of this book reflects that truth. Patti was gone before the shift ended—before the workday concluded, before anyone noticed something was wrong, before concern had time to turn into action. The ordinary rhythms of life continued uninterrupted, even as hers stopped.

This is how disappearances endure.

Not through chaos, but through quiet.

Adult women vanish this way more often than people realize. Their disappearances are easier to misinterpret, easier to delay responding to, easier to explain away. Autonomy becomes a shield behind which urgency fades. Assumptions fill the space where investigation should be.

Patti's case exposes how dangerous that gap can be.

By the time the alarm was raised, the most critical hours were already gone. Whatever had happened—whatever truth lay behind the promises, the money, the denial—had settled into silence.

And silence, once established, is hard to break.

This chapter is not about solving the case. It is about naming what happened in the only way that feels honest. Patti did not simply disappear. She was removed from her life at a moment when no one was watching closely enough to stop it.

Whether by deception, betrayal, or violence, the result is the same.

A mother never came home.

A son grew up without answers.

And a truth remains locked in the space between belief and proof.

Gone before the shift ended is not just a phrase.

It is the reality of Patti Adkins' last day.

A reminder that disappearances don't always announce themselves.

Sometimes, they slip quietly into the space between *now* and *later*—and never give back what they take.

EPILOGUE

— *Waiting for the Truth*

There are disappearances that become famous. And there are disappearances that simply become permanent.

falls into the second category—a woman who vanished without spectacle, without a national countdown, without the kind of sustained outrage that forces answers into daylight. Her story has lived for years in quiet places: in family conversations that trail off, in file folders that grow older, in the sharp pause that follows her name.

For her son, the disappearance did not become a chapter of the past. It became part of the structure of his life.

He grew up with a missing mother, which is different from grief and different from death. Death offers a certainty that can be mourned. Missing offers only an open door you never stop staring at, even when the room behind you changes and time moves forward without permission.

For Patti's family, time has not solved anything. It has only rearranged the questions.

Was she deceived?

Was she lured into a meeting she could not control?

Did someone panic and hide what happened?

Did someone plan it long before she ever withdrew money or clocked out early?

And perhaps the most painful question of all:

How did someone disappear so completely in the space of an ordinary afternoon?

The case remains unresolved, and that unresolved status shapes everything about the way it is carried. Patti's name does not belong to history. It belongs to waiting. Waiting for a call that never comes, waiting for a break that never arrives, waiting for the day someone finally decides silence costs more than truth.

Cold cases often survive on one fragile possibility: that time changes people.

It changes fear into fatigue.

It changes loyalty into resentment.

It changes guilt into something heavier.

And sometimes—sometimes—it turns a secret into a confession.

If Patti's disappearance involved another person, then someone has lived for years with knowledge they have not shared. It might be a direct truth, or it might be a single detail that never seemed important until the years made it impossible to ignore. Either way, the missing piece exists somewhere outside the file.

It always does.

What remains in Patti's story is not only mystery, but a lesson about how easily a life can slip through the cracks of assumption. Patti was an adult, so urgency softened. Patti mentioned a trip, so delay felt reasonable. Patti didn't leave behind a broken car or a dramatic scene, so the world didn't stop the way it would have for someone else.

But Patti was still a mother.

Still loved.

Still missing.

And that should have been enough.

This book does not offer closure, because Patti's family has not been given any. It offers something smaller, but necessary: a record. A refusal to let her become only a name in a forgotten file. A statement that her disappearance mattered, and still matters, because the story is unfinished.

Somewhere, there is a truth attached to June 29, 2001.

Somewhere, there is an explanation for why a woman clocked out early—and never came home.

And until that truth is spoken, Patti Adkins remains what she has been for decades:

Not gone from memory.

Gone from reach.

Waiting, still, for the moment the silence breaks.

A PERSONAL REQUEST

Thank you for reading **Gone Before the Shift Ended: The Unanswered Disappearance of Patti Adkins**.

If this book stayed with you, I would be deeply grateful if you left a review. Even choosing a star rating—without writing anything more—helps more than you might realize, because it signals to bookstores and platforms that this story matters and helps other readers find a careful, victim-centered account.

If you'd like to leave a review, you can visit the Amazon page here:

Gone Before the Shift Ended:The Unanswered Disappearance of Patti Adkins

Or simply scan the QR code below to go directly to the review page:

Your support helps keep the focus where it belongs—on Patti Adkins, her loved ones, and the unanswered questions that still deserve attention.

With gratitude,

Linda Davidson

THE GONE BEFORE SERIES

True Crime Disappearances at the Edge of Ordinary Time

Gone Before the Shift Ended: The Unanswered Disappearance of Patti Adkins

A factory worker vanishes after her night shift, leaving behind secrets, suspicion, and a case still clouded in silence.

Gone Before Morning: The Unanswered Case of Asha Degree

A nine-year-old girl walks into the dark before dawn — and is never seen again.

Gone Before Sunrise: The Disappearance of Holly Bobo

A young nursing student is led into the woods at daybreak, sparking one of Tennessee's most haunting investigations.

ALSO BY LINDA DAVIDSON

1. *The Last Flight: Neerja Bhanot's 17 Hours of Bravery That Saved 340 Lives*
2. *Broken Faith: The Crimes of the Lafferty Brothers*
3. *Blood in the Pulpit: The Killer Minister*
4. *Children of Doom: The Order of the Solar Temple*
5. *He Was Almost Home: The True Story of Jason Landry's Disappearance and the Miles That Vanished With Him*
6. *Deserted: The Mystery of Daniel Robinson in the Arizona Desert*
7. *Runaway or Taken? : The Mystery of Phoenix Coldon*
8. *The Devil in Cielo Drive : Inside Charles Manson's Cult of Fear*
9. *The Vanished Jogger : The Mystery of Mollie Tibbetts*
10. *The Doctor of Death: Harold Shipman and the Trust That Killed*
11. *Silent Campus : The Disappearance of Kristin Smart*
12. *Echoes at Fox Hollow: The Killer Next Door Herb Baumeister's Hidden Graves*
13. *The Silent Apartment: The Chicago Tylenol Murders That Changed Everything*
14. *Tracks in the Snow : The Strange Case of Amy Wroe Bechtel*
15. *No Footsteps Back: The Disappearance of Branson Perry*
16. *Trail of Silence: The Missing Case of Zebb Quinn*
17. *Lost in the Night: The Disappearance of Brian Shaffer*
18. *The Surgeon of Sin Inside the Twisted Mind and Crimes of Jack Wayne Rogers*
19. *The Vanished Girl: The Disappearance of Tara Calico and*

the Polaroid That Haunts
20. *Dark Road Exit: The Missing Case of Leah Roberts*

AUTHOR'S NOTE

This book is a work of narrative true crime. It is based on publicly available reporting, known timelines, and the limited verified facts accessible in an unresolved case. Where details are uncertain, disputed, or not publicly confirmed, the narrative reflects that uncertainty rather than forcing conclusions.

Some scenes are presented in a cohesive narrative style to help readers understand sequence, context, and emotional stakes. This does not mean the author claims access to private case files or undisclosed evidence. The goal is clarity, restraint, and respect —especially in a case where a family continues to live without closure.

If you have credible information about the disappearance of Patti Adkins, please contact the appropriate law enforcement agency.

ACKNOWLEDGMENTS

Some stories refuse to fade. *Gone Before the Shift Ended: The Unanswered Disappearance of Patti Adkins* exists because people refused to let Patti become a footnote—because they continued asking questions long after headlines stopped printing her name.

My deepest respect goes first to Patti Adkins and to the family and loved ones who have carried her absence every single day since she vanished. The weight of not knowing is its own kind of grief—one that does not settle, one that does not resolve. Their endurance, dignity, and insistence that Patti be remembered as more than a missing-person statistic shaped the heart of this book.

I am grateful to the journalists who preserved early reporting, even when the case received limited national attention. Local reporters, editors, and broadcasters documented details that might otherwise have disappeared with time. Their work provided an essential foundation for reconstructing events with accuracy and care.

Thank you to the investigators—past and present—who worked the case, reviewed evidence, revisited timelines, and kept the file from closing permanently. Cold cases demand patience, humility, and a willingness to admit uncertainty. Even when answers remain elusive, continued effort matters.

I also extend appreciation to archivists, librarians, and records clerks who safeguard court documents, public filings, and news archives. True crime writing depends not on rumor but on preserved documentation, and their often-unseen work makes responsible storytelling possible.

To the researchers and advocates who focus on missing persons cases—particularly those involving working-class women whose disappearances rarely command national urgency—your advocacy challenges the hierarchy of attention that too often determines which stories are amplified and which are neglected.

Finally, thank you to the readers who approach true crime with empathy rather than curiosity alone. If you are here, it means you believe stories like Patti's deserve to be examined with care, restraint, and accountability. It means you understand that behind every case file is a family still waiting.

This book was written not to sensationalize a mystery, but to honor a woman who went to work and never came home—and to acknowledge the unsettling truth that some disappearances remain unresolved not because they lack significance, but because they lack sustained attention.

May Patti Adkins never be reduced to a headline. May her name continue to be spoken.

DISCLAIMER

Gone Before the Shift Ended: The Unanswered Disappearance of Patti Adkins is a work of nonfiction based on publicly available records, archival news reporting, court documents, and other documented sources. Every reasonable effort has been made to verify facts at the time of writing. Any errors or omissions are the sole responsibility of the author.

This case remains unresolved. No individual has been convicted in connection with Patti Adkins' disappearance. Where persons are discussed in relation to the investigation, their involvement is presented as it appears in public records, media accounts, or official statements. Allegations, suspicions, or investigative theories are identified as such and should not be interpreted as findings of guilt. All individuals are presumed innocent unless proven guilty in a court of law.

Certain scenes in this book are reconstructed from multiple documented sources, including investigative timelines, interviews, and contemporaneous reporting. These reconstructions are intended to provide narrative clarity while remaining faithful to the known record. Dialogue is drawn from documented statements where available; minor edits for clarity or length do not alter meaning. Where precise details are unknown, that uncertainty is acknowledged.

To protect privacy and prevent unnecessary harm, some nonessential identifying details of private individuals may be limited or withheld. Such decisions do not alter the factual substance of the case.

This book addresses themes of disappearance, potential violence, and unresolved trauma. Reader discretion is advised. The intent of this work is not to sensationalize or exploit tragedy, but to examine the historical record thoughtfully and respectfully.

Nothing in this book constitutes legal advice, investigative guidance, or professional opinion. Discussions of law enforcement procedures, forensic limitations, or investigative decisions are presented for informational purposes only.

This is an independent journalistic and historical work. Any agencies, organizations, or institutions referenced herein do not endorse the author's conclusions or interpretations

NOTES ON APPROACH AND TERMINOLOGY

- **Confirmed**: Details supported by official statements or multiple reputable reports.
- **Reported**: Details described in media coverage or community accounts but not fully verified publicly.
- **Theory**: A proposed explanation that remains unproven.

In open cases, some information may be withheld by investigators to protect the integrity of ongoing work. This book respects that boundary and avoids naming private individuals as perpetrators without legal findings.

FOLLOW THE AUTHOR

To explore all of Linda Davidson's books and new releases, visit her Amazon Author Page on Kindle: Linda Davidson.

END NOTE

— *Light in the Dark*

Stories like this one walk us through some of the darkest places a human heart can go. It is easy to believe that evil has the last word—that violence, corruption, or indifference are stronger than anything else.

The Bible says something different. It tells us that God sees every unseen hurt, hears every unheard prayer, and judges every hidden deed. It also says that no life is beyond His reach, and no story is too broken to be redeemed. Justice matters to God. So does mercy. So does you.

If what you've read has stirred fear, anger, or regret in your own heart, know this: the door back to Him is never closed. Repentance is simply turning around and letting Him meet you where you are.

"Do not be overcome by evil, but overcome evil with good."

— Romans 12:21

"The light shines in the darkness, and the darkness has not overcome it."

—John 1:5

May these pages not only expose what went wrong, but also awaken a hunger for what is right—for justice, for truth, and for the kind of grace that can still save a soul.

ABOUT THE AUTHOR

Linda Davidson is a true crime author who writes for readers who want more than shock value — they want truth with a heartbeat.

She focuses on the kinds of stories that stay with you long after the news cameras leave: unsolved murders, missing persons, rural disappearances, and investigations that never received clear answers. Instead of chasing sensational headlines, Linda writes with one question in mind: *How can I honor the victim and still tell the full truth of what happened?*

In each book, she blends careful research, clear timelines, and compassionate storytelling. Readers are guided through evidence, leads, theories, and dead ends in a way that is easy to follow and emotionally grounded. Her work keeps the victim at the center of the narrative while also examining the failures, gaps, and human decisions that shaped each case.

Linda's books are written for true crime readers who care about people, not just plot twists. She writes for those who feel frustrated by shallow coverage and are hungry for deeper, more thoughtful explorations of the cases that haunt them.

Her promise is simple:

She will research carefully.

She will explain clearly.

She will tell the truth with respect.

She will never forget that the people she writes about were real.

Linda Davidson is a true crime author dedicated to telling

the stories others forget. She writes about unsolved murders, mysterious disappearances, and cold cases with a focus on the victims, their families, and the communities left behind. Combining deep research with compassionate storytelling, she helps readers make sense of complex investigations without losing sight of the human beings at the center of every case.

A FINAL WORD TO THE READER

If you've reached the end of this book, you've carried Patti Adkins' name for a while. That matters.

Unresolved disappearances rely on memory—on people who refuse to let the story sink into silence. Sometimes a case changes because of one conversation finally revisited, one detail finally spoken, one person finally deciding the truth is worth the cost.

Patti was not a mystery first. She was a mother. A worker. A person with a life that should have continued past an ordinary Friday afternoon.

If you know something—anything—about what happened after she clocked out early, please consider coming forward. Even small details can matter more than you think.

Some stories remain unfinished not because the truth is unknowable—but because it hasn't been said yet.

REFERENCES

ABC 6 On Your Side. (2025, May 19). Search for Patti Adkins intensifies 24 years after disappearance in Union County.

Charley Project. (n.d.). Patricia Ann Adkins. (Retrieved February 10, 2026)

Marysville Journal-Tribune. (2025, July 7). Adkins case remains a priority.

National Missing and Unidentified Persons System. (n.d.). Missing Person Case: Patricia A. Adkins (NamUs #MP1665). (Retrieved February 10, 2026)

Ohio Attorney General. (n.d.). Missing Adult – Patricia Ann Adkins. (Retrieved February 10, 2026)

Union County Sheriff's Office (Ohio). (2015). Patricia "Patti" Adkins Case #01-F-834 (case flyer).

Union County Sheriff's Office (Ohio), Investigations Division. (2023, June 28). Unsolved cold case: Missing person/homicide—Patricia "Patti" Adkins (Case #01-F-834).

Union County Daily Digital. (2023, June 29). Today marks 22nd anniversary of Patti Adkins disappearance.

Yahoo News. (2025, July 20). Disappearance of Union County woman from Honda plant remains unsolved.

Crime Junkie. (n.d.). MISSING: Patti Adkins. *audiochuck*. (Retrieved February 10, 2026)

FURTHER READING AND VIEWING

Adkins, P. A. (n.d.). Missing Person Case: Patricia A. Adkins (NamUs #MP1665). *National Missing and Unidentified Persons System*. (Retrieved February 10, 2026)

Charley Project. (n.d.). Patricia Ann Adkins. *The Charley Project*. (Retrieved February 10, 2026)

Union County Sheriff's Office (Ohio), Investigations Division. (2023, June 28). Unsolved cold case: Missing person/homicide—Patricia "Patti" Adkins (Case #01-F-834). *Union County, Ohio*.

ABC 6 On Your Side. (2025, May 19). Search for Patti Adkins intensifies 24 years after disappearance in Union County. *ABC 6 On Your Side*.

Marysville Journal-Tribune. (2025, July 7). Adkins case remains a priority. *Marysville Journal-Tribune*.

FURTHER VIEWING

Disappeared. (2011, January 10). **Secret Rendezvous** (Season 3, Episode 2) [TV episode]. *Investigation Discovery*. Available on Apple TV: https://tv.apple.com/us/episode/secret-rendezvous/umc.cmc.3dmlvj1yejmojkc8peyj9plba?showId=umc.cmc.25ga0ob0e1w346fqz4b7iuhs1

Disappeared. (2011, January 10). **Secret Rendezvous** (Season 3, Episode 2) [TV episode]. *Investigation Discovery*. Available on Max: https://www.hbomax.com/ky/en/shows/disappeared/s3/aac3db5f-d804-4388-bba9-0e4e4ca6ee1a/e2-secret-rendezvous/2ccbec48-e462-48e5-bb0d-00e07f91ab93

YouTube. (n.d.). WHEN PATTI ADKINS NEVER CAME HOME | A CraftTime…. (Retrieved February 10, 2026)

YouTube. (n.d.). Where is Patti Adkins? Ohio woman vanishes after secret trip. (Retrieved February 10, 2026)

FURTHER LISTENING (PODCASTS)

Crime Junkie. (2019, May 20). MISSING: Patti Adkins. *audiochuck*.

Crime Junkie. (2019, May 20). MISSING: Patti Adkins (Spotify episode). *Spotify*.

The Murder Diaries. (2025, December 11). MURDERED: Patti Adkins. *The Murder Diaries Podcast*.

Gone Before the Shift Ended follows the last known hours of Patti's life and the investigation that stalled in silence, leaving her family with questions that still haven't been answered.

Some disappearances don't happen in the dark.

They happen while the world is still working.

APPENDIX A — TIMELINE AT A GLANCE

Before June 29, 2001

- Patti Adkins is living in Marysville, Ohio, working at a Honda supplier plant.
- She is a devoted mother with stable routines.
- She is involved in a secret relationship with a married coworker.
- She withdraws a significant amount of cash shortly before her disappearance.

Friday, June 29, 2001

- Patti reports to work as usual.
- During her shift, she tells coworkers she is leaving early to go out of town for a few days.
- Patti clocks out early and leaves the workplace.
- **This is the last confirmed sighting of Patti Adkins.**

After June 29, 2001

- Patti does not return home and does not contact family or friends.
- Concern rises as the "short trip" explanation collapses.
- A missing person report is filed and law enforcement begins interviews and record checks.
- The man Patti believed she was traveling with denies the trip existed.
- Patti's accounts and phone activity go silent; no verified sightings follow.

Long-Term
- No body is recovered.
- No confirmed crime scene is identified.
- No arrests are made.
- The case remains open.

APPENDIX B — KEY PEOPLE AND RELATIONSHIPS

Patti Adkins
- Mother, employee, missing since June 29, 2001.
- Known for reliability, routine, and strong ties to her child.

Patti's Son
- Central to understanding why a voluntary disappearance is unlikely.
- The primary life impacted by Patti's unresolved absence.

Family Members
- The earliest advocates pushing back against "adult choice" assumptions.
- Continued efforts to keep Patti's name present and her case active.

The Married Coworker / Boyfriend
- The person Patti reportedly believed she was traveling with.
- Denies the trip and is a focal point of scrutiny.
- No charges filed.

Coworkers
- Provide the last known confirmations of Patti's plan and early departure.
- Help establish that Patti expected to return.

Law Enforcement

- Investigates within the limits of a case without a confirmed scene or definitive evidence of foul play.

APPENDIX C — MYTHS VS. FACTS

Myth: "She was just a runaway."

Fact: Patti was an adult, but she was also a devoted mother who left no arrangements for her child and left behind most of her life.

Myth: "The cash withdrawal proves she planned to disappear."

Fact: The withdrawal is suspicious, but it doesn't match the scale or preparation typical of someone starting over permanently.

Myth: "There's no reason to suspect foul play without a body."

Fact: Many homicide cases begin without a body. Lack of remains is not proof of safety—only proof of missing evidence.

Myth: "If the boyfriend denied the trip, Patti must have made it up."

Fact: Multiple coworkers reported Patti said she was traveling. The contradiction is central—and unresolved.

Myth: "The case is cold, so it must be hopeless."

Fact: Cold cases are solved every year through confessions, renewed forensic testing, and witnesses speaking later.

APPENDIX D — HOW WORKPLACE DISAPPEARANCES GO COLD

Workplace disappearances often stall for predictable reasons:

1) Adults are assumed to have left by choice

Early urgency can be delayed, which is costly.

2) The last confirmed location is "ordinary"

A workplace isn't automatically treated as a crime scene.

3) Evidence evaporates quickly

If the disappearance happens off-site, evidence may never be preserved.

4) Investigations depend on verifiable data

Without a vehicle, a scene, or digital trail, the case becomes witness-based—and vulnerable to silence.

5) Relationships complicate reporting

Affairs, secrecy, and reputation concerns can delay honesty and reduce cooperation.

6) Time erodes memories and leverage

Details blur, records vanish, and people move on.

APPENDIX E — APPEAL FOR INFORMATION

The disappearance of remains unresolved.

If you have any information—no matter how small—about Patti Adkins' disappearance, consider contacting law enforcement. Even details that seem minor can become critical when combined with other information.

You may have:

- Heard a conversation about a trip that was planned
- Known someone who mentioned Patti's disappearance privately
- Noticed unusual behavior or a sudden change in someone close to the case
- Seen or heard something in late June or early July 2001 that didn't make sense until later
- Held back information out of fear, uncertainty, or loyalty

Time does not erase truth. It often increases its weight.

How to Report Information

Contact the appropriate local law enforcement agency connected to Marysville, Ohio, or the county jurisdiction handling the case.

If you are unsure whether your information matters, report it anyway.

Let investigators decide.

Printed in Dunstable, United Kingdom